CLB 1488
© 1986 Colour Library Books Ltd., Godalming, Surrey, England
All rights reserved
This edition published in 1993 by SMITHMARK Publishers Inc.,
16 East 32nd Street, New York, NY 10016
SMITHMARK books are available for bulk purchase for sales promotion
and premium use. For details write or call the manager of special sales,
SMITHMARK Publishers Inc., 16 East 32nd Street,
New York, NY 10016; (212) 532-6600.
ISBN 0-8317-6804-5
Printed in Singapore

TEXT BY
Carolyn Garner

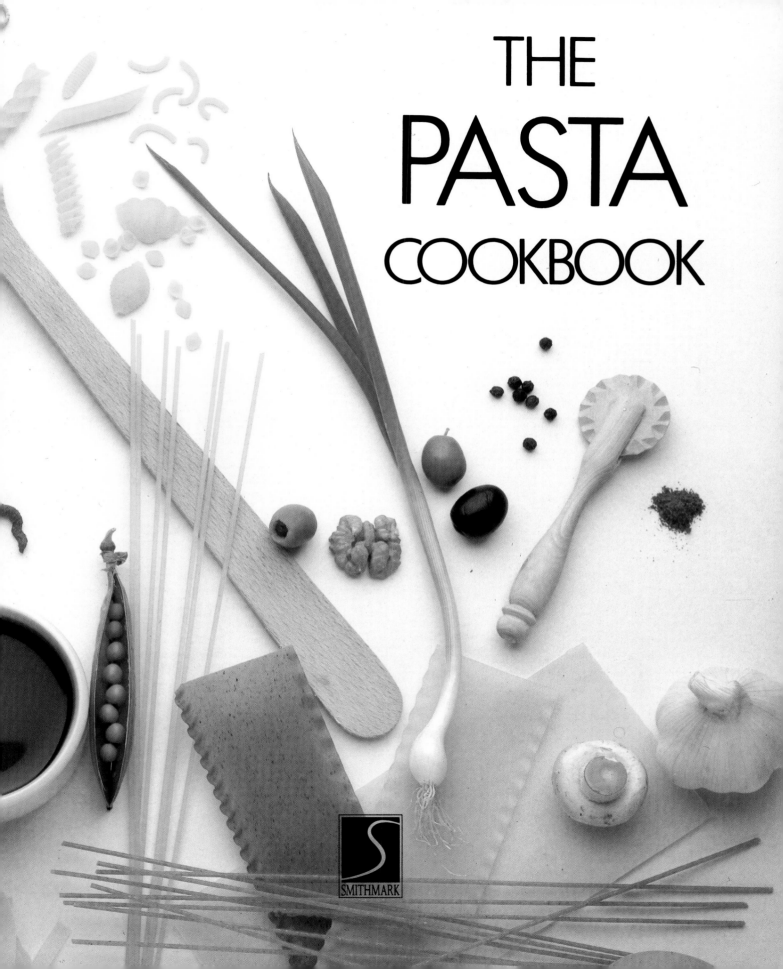

THE
PASTA
COOKBOOK

SMITHMARK

 Contents

Introduction

Pasta: one of the world's most basic yet versatile foods.

With the increased migration of people and ideas, and a greater interest in foods of other nations, it is no surprise that pasta cookery has become so fashionable.

The increased demand, having resulted in the availability of necessary ingredients, means that the enthusiastic cook can launch into myriad culinary adventures with "pasta" – the chameleon of the cookery world.

Although chiefly an Italian product, pasta has become an ubiquitous term, with the cuisines of many other countries often including noodles.

Pasta is literally a paste made with flour and eggs. Commercial pasta is made from a hard wheat called durum wheat, but fresh pasta may be made with any kind of flour. It is sometimes made in different colors, green (pasta verde) with the addition of spinach; and pink (pasta rosa) which has tomato paste added, to name just a couple. Pasta is now readily available dried and fresh, or can be made in the home with some practice.

It takes little time to cook and should on no account be overcooked as there is nothing worse than a congealed mass of pasta. Always use a large, uncovered saucepan, lots of boiling salted water and a few drops of oil to separate the pasta and prevent the water boiling over. The water should not be boiling too rapidly and a careful stir will also help prevent the pasta from sticking together. The pasta will be ready when tender but still firm, or "al dente" – firm to the bite.

Pour immediately into a colander to prevent further cooking, and rinse under hot water to remove any excess starch. It should then be served immediately. However, if it needs to be kept, put it in a bowl of hand-hot water until needed.

The longer pastas, such as spaghetti, should be held at one end and put into rapidly boiling water, gently coiled around the pan as it softens, then simmered until "al dente". It should not be broken up.

Fresh pasta cooks a lot quicker than dried pasta. Wholemeal pasta takes longer, and the cooking time will vary a lot according to the thickness of the pasta type.

The amount of pasta per person will vary according to circumstances – individual appetites, and what the pasta is being served with, must play a leading part in how much should be cooked.

There are a great many pasta shapes, and their Italian names often differ from one region to another. It may, therefore, be prudent to search for the shape of the less known varieties of pasta rather than to try to memorize the names.

The most common ingredients used are tomatoes (generally Italian plum tomatoes), onions, mushrooms and Parmesan cheese. However, I would like to mention a few important ingredients. Of the cheeses, Parmesan (Parmigiano), pecorino and ricotta are most frequently used. Parmesan cheese is made from cow's milk and is used for grating and cooking, as it melts well without becoming stringy. Pecorino, a sheep's milk cheese, is also used for grating and, with a sharper flavor than Parmesan cheese, heightens the spicy dishes. Ricotta, a fresh, unripened cheese, is made from the whey of cow's milk. As it is smooth and has a mild taste it is used in a number of savory and sweet dishes.

Of course, one fundamental ingredient that must be mentioned here is olive oil. The distinct flavor of the green olive has enhanced many a pasta dish. Good olive oil is a greeny-yellow in color, the best variety being the first pressing or virgin olive oil.

Tortellini with Mushroom Sauce (right) and Ravioli with Ricotta Cheese (top right).

Soups and Elegant Appetizers

Chick-Pea Soup

PREPARATION TIME: Chick-peas soaked overnight plus 5 minutes

COOKING TIME: 1 hour 20 minutes

1 cup dried chick-peas
1 cup soup pasta
2 cloves garlic
3 tbsps olive oil
1 tsp basil
1½ cups plum tomatoes, chopped
3 cups water
1 chicken bouillon cube
2 tbsps Parmesan cheese, grated
Salt and pepper

Soak chick-peas overnight in enough water to cover by 1 inch. Discard water in which the chick-peas have soaked. Place the chick-peas in a large, heavy pan, and cover with 1 inch of water. Bring to the boil and simmer, covered, for about 1 hour until chick-peas are tender, ensuring that they do not boil dry. Heat olive oil in a heavy pan, and sauté garlic cloves. When browned, remove and discard garlic cloves. Add tomatoes and their juice, water and basil, and cook together for 20 minutes. Add drained chick-peas, crumbled bouillon cube, and salt and pepper to taste. Stir well; simmer a further 10 minutes. Bring back to boil. Add pasta, and cook, stirring frequently, for 10 minutes. Mix in half of the Parmesan cheese. Adjust seasoning, and serve immediately, with remaining Parmesan cheese sprinkled on top. Serves 4.
Note: Soup may be puréed before pasta is added, if desired.

Tagliatelle with Egg and Caviar

PREPARATION TIME: 5 minutes

COOKING TIME: 15 minutes

½ pound red tagliatelle
1 small jar red salmon caviar or lumpfish roe
4 small eggs, hard boiled
4 tbsps butter or margarine
Black pepper

Put eggs into boiling water and cook for 12 minutes. Rinse under

cold water, to stop further cooking. Remove shells, cut in half, and scoop out yolks with a teaspoon. Push yolks through a strainer. Wash egg-whites, and cut into strips. Set aside. Cook tagliatelle in plenty of boiling salted water until *al dente*. Rinse in hot water, and drain well. Heat butter in pan, add freshly-ground black pepper and tagliatelle. Add egg whites, and toss well. Sprinkle caviar over, and top with egg-yolk. Serve immediately. Serves 4 as a starter.

Minestra

PREPARATION TIME: 15 minutes

COOKING TIME: 45 minutes

¾ cup short-cut/elbow macaroni
2 tbsps olive oil
1 onion
1 carrot
1 stick celery
1½ quarts water
½ pound fresh spinach
2 tomatoes
1 tsp rosemary
2 tbsps chopped parsley
2 cloves garlic, crushed
¼ cup Parmesan cheese, grated
Salt and pepper

Cut onion, carrot and celery into thick matchstick strips. Heat oil in a large, heavy pan, and fry vegetable strips until just browning, stirring occasionally. Pour on water, add salt and pepper, and let simmer for 20 minutes. Meanwhile, wash and cut spinach leaves into shreds, add to soup and cook for 10 minutes. Scald and skin tomatoes, and chop roughly, removing seeds. Add tomatoes, macaroni, garlic, parsley and rosemary to the soup, and simmer a further 10 minutes. Adjust seasoning. Serve with grated Parmesan cheese if desired.

Meatball Soup

PREPARATION TIME: 10 minutes

COOKING TIME: 1 hour 40 minutes

OVEN: 350°F (180°C)

½ pound ground minced beef
¼ cup breadcrumbs
1 egg, beaten
1 pound beef bones
1 stick celery
1 carrot
1 onion
1 tbsp oil
1 can tomato sauce
¾ cup soup pasta
1 tbsp chopped parsley
Salt and pepper

Place bones, peeled carrot, onion and celery in a large saucepan and cover with cold water. Bring to the boil: cover and simmer for one hour at least. Meanwhile, mix together lightly beaten egg with ground beef, breadcrumbs and plenty of seasoning. Roll a teaspoon amount into small balls and place on a roasting pan with the oil. Bake in a preheated oven for 45 minutes, turning occasionally. Strain stock into a saucepan. Add tomato sauce to the stock. Bring to the boil, and simmer for 15 minutes. Add pasta and cook for 10 minutes, stirring frequently. Add meatballs, adjust seasoning, and stir in chopped parsley. Serve hot.

This page: Tagliatelle with Egg and Caviar.

Facing page: Minestra (top), Meatball Soup (center right) and Chick-Pea Soup (bottom).

Tomato Soup

| **PREPARATION TIME:** 15 minutes |
| **COOKING TIME:** 45 minutes |

1 cup short-cut/elbow macaroni
2 tbsps butter or margarine
1 small onion, peeled and chopped
1 small green pepper, cored, seeds
  removed, and chopped
1 tbsp flour
1 quart brown stock, or water plus 2
  beef bouillon cubes
1 pound tomatoes, chopped
2 tbsps tomato paste
1 tbsp grated horseradish
Salt and pepper

Garnish:

2 tbsps soured cream,
1 tbsp chopped parsley

Heat the butter in a pan. Cover and
cook the onion and green pepper
for 5 minutes. Add the flour and
stir. Add stock, tomatoes and
tomato paste. Simmer for 15
minutes. Purée soup and strain.
Return to pan, and season with salt
and pepper to taste. Add macaroni
10 minutes before serving. Simmer
and stir occasionally. Add horseradish before serving. Garnish with
soured cream and parsley. Serve
immediately.

Tagliatelle with Smoked Salmon and Caviar

| **PREPARATION TIME:** 5 minutes |
| **COOKING TIME:** 15 minutes |

½ pound green tagliatelle
¼ pound smoked salmon, cut into
  strips
Juice of half a lemon
2 tbsps red salmon caviar or lumpfish
  roe
2 tbsps butter or margarine
2 tbsps heavy cream
Black pepper

Garnish:

Lemon slices

Cook tagliatelle in lots of boiling
salted water for 10 minutes, or until
tender but still firm. Rinse under
hot water, and drain well. Heat
butter in pan, and add lemon juice
and freshly-ground black pepper.
Return tagliatelle to pan, and add
smoked salmon. Toss together.
Serve topped with heavy cream
and a sprinkling of red caviar.
Garnish with lemon slices. Serve
immediately. Serves 4 as a starter.

Tagliatelle with Smoked Salmon and Caviar (top left), Shell Pasta with Taramasalata (left). Top picture: Bean Soup (top) and Tomato Soup (bottom).

Shell Pasta with Taramasalata

| **PREPARATION TIME:** 15 minutes |
| **COOKING TIME:** 15 minutes |

1 9oz package shell pasta
1 cup taramasalata
2 tbsps lemon juice
10 black olives, pips removed, and
  chopped
1 tbsp black caviar or lumpfish roe

To Make Taramasalata:

½ cup smoked salmon roe
Half onion, grated
8 slices white bread, crusts removed
4 tbsps milk
⅓ cup olive oil
2 tsps lemon juice
Black pepper

Crumble bread into a bowl and
add milk. Set aside to soak. Scoop
the salmon roe out of its skin, and
break it down with a wooden
spoon. Squeeze the bread dry in a
strainer. Add onion and bread to
salmon roe, and mix well. Add oil
and lemon juice very gradually,
alternating between the two. Beat
until smooth and creamy. Add
pepper to taste, and salt if
necessary. Cook pasta shells in lots
of boiling salted water for 10
minutes or until *al dente*. Rinse in
hot water, and drain well. Sprinkle
over lemon juice; toss together
with taramasalata, and garnish with
caviar and black olives. Serve
immediately. Serves 4 as a starter.

Bean Soup

| **PREPARATION TIME:** 15 minutes |
| **COOKING TIME:** 1 hour 45 minutes |

1 15oz can kidney beans
2 strips bacon, chopped
1 stick celery, chopped
1 small onion, peeled and chopped
1 clove garlic, crushed
½ cup plum tomatoes, chopped and
  seeds removed
4 cups water
1 chicken bouillon cube
1 tbsp chopped parsley
1 tsp basil
1 cup whole-wheat ring pasta
Salt and pepper

Place kidney beans, bacon, celery,
onion, garlic, parsley, basil,
tomatoes and water in a large pan.
Bring to the boil and add bouillon
cube and salt and pepper to taste.
Cover and cook over a low heat for
about 1½ hours. Raise heat and add
pasta, stirring well. Stir frequently
until pasta is cooked but still firm –
about 10 minutes. Serve
immediately.

Seafood

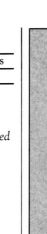

Spaghetti Marinara

PREPARATION TIME: 10 minutes

COOKING TIME: 20 minutes

1 9oz package spaghetti
1 pound shrimp, shelled and
    de-veined
½ pound scallops, cleaned and sliced
6-8 anchovies
1 large can (about 2 cups) plum
    tomatoes, seeded and chopped
½ cup dry white wine
½ cup water
1 bay leaf
4 peppercorns
2 tbsps olive oil
1 tsp basil
2 cloves garlic, crushed
1 tbsp tomato paste
1 tbsp chopped parsley
Salt and pepper

Drain anchovies and cut into small
pieces. Place water, wine, bay leaf
and peppercorns in a pan. Heat to a
slow boil. Add scallops and cook
for 2 minutes. Remove and drain.
Heat the oil, add garlic and basil,
and cook for 30 seconds. Add
tomatoes, anchovies and tomato
paste. Stir until combined. Cook
for 10 minutes. Meanwhile, cook
the spaghetti in a large pan of
boiling salted water for 10 minutes,
or until tender but still firm. Drain.
Add seafood to sauce, and cook a
further 1 minute. Add parsley and
stir through. Season with salt and
pepper to taste. Toss gently. Pour
sauce over spaghetti and serve
immediately, sprinkled with parsley.

Pasta Shells with
Seafood

PREPARATION TIME: 5 minutes

COOKING TIME: 15 minutes

1 9oz package pasta shells
1 pound shrimp, shelled and
    de-veined
¼ pound scallops, cleaned and sliced
4 tbsps butter or margarine
2 cloves garlic, crushed
½ cup dry white wine

1 cup cream
2 tbsps water
1 tbsp cornstarch
1 tbsp lemon juice
1 tbsp chopped parsley
Salt and pepper

Melt butter in a pan. Add garlic,
and cook for 1 minute. Add wine
and cream, and bring back to boil,
and cook 2 minutes. Slake cornstarch with the water, and pour into
sauce. Stir until boiling. Add lemon
juice and salt and pepper to taste.
Meanwhile, cook the pasta in
plenty of boiling salted water, until
tender – about 10 minutes. Drain,
shaking to remove excess water.
Add shrimp and scallops to sauce
and cook 3 minutes. Pour over
pasta shells, toss, and garnish with
parsley.

Vermicelli Pescatore

PREPARATION TIME: 15 minutes

COOKING TIME: 40 minutes

¼ pint mussels
¼ pint clams
½ pound cod fish fillets
¼ pound squid, cleaned
4 Gulf shrimp, cooked
4 fresh oysters, cooked
1 9oz package vermicelli
1 cup dry white wine
¼ cup olive oil
4 small cans (about 4 cups) tomato
    sauce
2 tbsps tomato paste
Half a green pepper, diced

Prepare seafood. If using fresh
mussels, clean closed mussels,
removing beard, and cook in

boiling water for 3 minutes until
they open. (Discard any that
remain closed). Cool and remove
from shells, keeping a few in shells
for garnish if desired. Skin and bone
fillets, and cut fish into ½ inch
pieces. Clean squid and cut into
rings. Heat 2 tbsps oil in a pan, and
add the squid. Fry gently until
golden brown, then add wine,
tomato, green pepper, and salt and
pepper to taste. Simmer for 20
minutes then add fish. Simmer for
a further 10 minutes, stirring
occasionally. Add clams and
mussels and, when mixture reboils,
adjust seasoning. Meanwhile, cook
spaghetti in lots of boiling salted
water for 10 minutes, or until
tender but still firm. Drain well.
Add seafood, and toss. Garnish
with shrimp and fresh oysters.

Sauces and Hearty Eating

Facing page: Farfalle with Beef, Mushroom and Soured Cream (top), Tagliatelle Carbonara (center left) and Pasta Spirals with Spinach and Bacon (bottom).

Tortiglioni alla Puttanesca

PREPARATION TIME: 10 minutes

COOKING TIME: 15 minutes

SERVES: 4 people

1 9oz package tortiglioni, spiral pasta
1 small can (about 1 cup) plum tomatoes, drained
6-8 anchovy fillets
2 tbsps olive oil
2 cloves garlic, crushed
½ tsp basil
Pinch chili powder
½ cup black olives, stoned and chopped
2 tbsps chopped parsley
Salt
Pepper

Chop tomatoes and remove seeds, and chop anchovies. Cook pasta in plenty of boiling salted water for 10 minutes, or until tender but still firm. Rinse in hot water, and drain. Pour into a warmed bowl. Meanwhile, heat oil in pan, add garlic, chili powder and basil, and cook for 1 minute. Add tomatoes, parsley, olives and anchovies, and cook for a few minutes. Season with salt and pepper. Pour sauce over pasta, and mix together thoroughly. Serve immediately.

Pasta Spirals with Spinach and Bacon

PREPARATION TIME: 15 minutes

COOKING TIME: 15 minutes

1 9oz package pasta spirals
½ pound spinach
¼ pound Canadian bacon
1 clove garlic, crushed
1 small red chili pepper
½ small sweet red pepper
1 small onion
3 tbsps olive oil
Salt and pepper

Wash spinach, remove stalks and cut into thin shreds. Core and seed pepper, and slice half finely. Peel onion and chop finely. Chop the bacon. Remove seeds from chili pepper, and slice thinly. Cook pasta spirals in plenty of boiling salted water for 10 minutes, or until tender but still firm. Drain. Meanwhile, heat oil in pan, and add garlic, onion, bacon, chili pepper and sweet red pepper. Fry for 2 minutes, add spinach, and fry for a further 2 minutes, stirring continuously. Season with salt and pepper to taste. Toss with pasta spirals. Serve immediately.

Tagliatelle Carbonara

PREPARATION TIME: 10 minutes

COOKING TIME: 15 minutes

1 9oz package tagliatelle
2 tbsps butter or margarine
8 strips bacon, shredded
1 tbsp olive oil
⅓ cup cream
Pinch of paprika
¼ cup Parmesan cheese, grated
2 eggs
Salt and pepper

This page: Tortiglioni alla Puttanesca.

Heat oil in a frying-pan, and cook bacon over a moderate heat until browning. Add paprika and cook for 1 minute. Add cream, and stir. Beat together eggs and grated cheese. Meanwhile, cook tagliatelle in lots of boiling salted water for 10 minutes, or until tender but still firm. Drain, return to pan with butter and black pepper, and toss. Add bacon mixture and egg mixture, and toss together. Add salt to taste. Serve immediately.

Farfalle with Beef, Mushroom and Soured Cream

PREPARATION TIME: 10 minutes

COOKING TIME: 15 minutes

1 9oz package farfalle (pasta butterflies – bows)
½ pound sirloin or butt steak, sliced
¼ cup mushrooms, sliced
¼ cup soured cream
10 green olives, stoned and chopped
1 onion, peeled and sliced
2 tbsps unsalted butter
1 tbsp flour
Salt and pepper

Garnish:
Soured cream
1 tbsp chopped parsley

With a very sharp knife, cut meat into narrow, short strips. Heat half the butter, and fry meat over a high heat until well browned. Set aside. Heat remaining butter in pan, and gently fry onion until soft and just beginning to color. Add mushrooms, and cook for 3 minutes. Stir in flour and continue frying for a further 3 minutes. Gradually stir in soured cream. When fully incorporated, add meat, olives, and salt and pepper to taste. Meanwhile, cook farfalle in plenty of boiling salted water for 10 minutes, or until tender but still firm. Drain well. Serve with beef and mushroom sauce on top. Garnish with a little extra soured cream and chopped parsley.

Penne with Anchovy Sauce

PREPARATION TIME: 5 minutes

COOKING TIME: 20 minutes

1 9oz package penne
6-8 anchovies

2 small cans (about 2 cups) tomato sauce
2 tbsps olive oil
3 tbsps chopped parsley
¼ cup Parmesan cheese, grated
2 tbsps butter or margarine
Pepper

Chop anchovies and cook them in the oil, stirring to a paste. Add tomato sauce to anchovies, with parsley and freshly-ground black pepper to taste. Bring to the boil and simmer, uncovered, for 10 minutes. Meanwhile, cook the penne in lots of boiling salted water for 10 minutes, or until tender but still firm. Rinse in hot water and drain well. Toss in butter. Combine sauce with the pasta, and sprinkle with parsley, and serve with Parmesan cheese. Serve immediately.

Whole-wheat Spaghetti with Peas and Bacon

PREPARATION TIME: 10 minutes

COOKING TIME: 15 minutes

1 9oz package whole-wheat spaghetti
1½ cups peas
1 tsp sugar
8 strips bacon, diced
4 tbsps butter or margarine
Salt and pepper

Garnish:
Parsley

Cook spaghetti in lots of boiling salted water for 10 minutes, or until tender but still firm. Drain. Meanwhile, cook peas in boiling water with a pinch of salt and a teaspoon of sugar. Melt butter in a pan, and fry bacon. When crisp, add peas, and salt and pepper to taste, and pour over spaghetti. Toss through, and serve immediately garnished with chopped parsley if desired.

Penne with Anchovy Sauce (left) and Whole-wheat Spaghetti with Peas and Bacon (below).

Spaghetti Neapolitana

PREPARATION TIME: 5 minutes

COOKING TIME: 30 minutes

SERVES: 4 people

1 pound spaghetti
2 small cans (about 2 cups tomato
    sauce)
2 tbsps olive oil
½ tsp oregano or marjoram
Salt
Pepper
2 tbsps chopped parsley
Parmesan cheese, grated

Heat oil in pan. Add oregano or marjoram, and cook for 30 seconds. Add tomato sauce, and salt and pepper. Bring to boil; reduce heat; simmer uncovered for 20-30 minutes. Meanwhile, cook spaghetti in lots of boiling salted water for about 10 minutes, or until tender but still firm. Rinse under hot water, and drain well. Pour tomato sauce over spaghetti, and toss gently. Sprinkle parsley over the top. Serve with Parmesan cheese. Serve immediately.

Spaghetti with Tomato, Salami and Green Olives

PREPARATION TIME: 15 minutes

COOKING TIME: 15 minutes

1 9oz package spaghetti
2 small cans (about 2 cups) tomato
    sauce
⅓ pound salami, sliced and shredded
1 cup green olives, stoned and
    chopped

1 clove garlic, crushed
2 tbsps olive oil
½ tbsp oregano
¼ cup pecorino cheese, grated
Salt and pepper

This page: Spaghetti with Tomato, Salami and Green Olives.

Facing page: Spaghetti Neapolitana (top) and Farfalle with Creamy Cheese Sauce (bottom).

Combine tomato sauce, oregano, salami and olives in a saucepan and heat gently. Add salt and pepper to taste. Meanwhile, cook spaghetti in plenty of boiling salted water for 10 minutes, or until tender but still firm. Drain well. Heat olive oil and freshly-ground black pepper in the pan used to cook the spaghetti. Add spaghetti, and pour the sauce over. Toss well. Serve immediately with pecorino cheese.

Farfalle with Creamy Cheese Sauce

PREPARATION TIME: 5 minutes

COOKING TIME: 15 minutes

SERVES: 4 people

1 9oz package farfalle (pasta
  butterflies / bows)
2 tbsps butter or margarine
2 tbsps flour
1 cup milk
¼ cup Gruyère or Cheddar cheese,
  grated
½ tsp Dijon mustard
1 tbsp grated Parmesan cheese

Heat butter in pan. Stir in flour and cook for 1 minute. Remove from heat and gradually stir in milk. Return to heat and stir continuously. Boil for 3 minutes. Stir in Gruyère or Cheddar cheese, and mustard; do not reboil. Meanwhile, cook the pasta in lots of boiling salted water for 10 minutes, or until tender but still firm. Rinse in hot water and drain well. Pour over cheese sauce, and toss. Top with a sprinkling of Parmesan cheese. Serve immediately.

Pasta with Tomato and Yogurt Sauce

PREPARATION TIME: 5 minutes

COOKING TIME: 40 minutes

1 9oz box pasta shells
⅓ cup plain yogurt
1 tbsp butter or margarine
1 tbsp flour
½ cup beef stock
2 small cans tomato sauce
1 bay leaf
Sprig of thyme
Parsley stalks
Salt and pepper

Melt butter in a pan. Stir in the flour, and pour in the stock gradually. Add tomato sauce, bay leaf, thyme and parsley stalks.

Season with salt and pepper. Bring to the boil, and simmer for 30 minutes. Adjust seasoning. Meanwhile, cook pasta in plenty of boiling salted water for 10 minutes, or until tender but still firm. Rinse in hot water and drain well. Place in warmed serving dish; pour over tomato sauce, then yogurt. (Yogurt may be marbled through tomato sauce). Serve immediately.

Penne with Chili Sauce

PREPARATION TIME: 40 minutes

COOKING TIME: 20 minutes

1 9oz package penne
1 clove garlic, crushed
1 onion, peeled and chopped
1 pound ripe tomatoes
1 eggplant
1 red chili pepper
2 tbsps oil
¼ cup pecorino cheese, grated

Trim and cut eggplant into ½ inch slices, and salt lightly. Leave for 30 minutes. Rinse and wipe dry with absorbent paper. Meanwhile, heat oil in a frying-pan over a moderate heat, and fry garlic and onion until lightly colored. Peel and seed tomatoes, and chop roughly. Seed chili pepper, and chop finely. Cut eggplant roughly and add to onion. Fry together for 5 minutes. Add tomatoes and chili pepper, and mix well. Simmer sauce gently, uncovered, for 5 minutes, stirring occasionally. Meanwhile, cook pasta in lots of boiling salted water for 10 minutes, or until tender but still firm, stirring occasionally. Rinse in hot water, and drain well. Place in a warmed serving dish. Add hot sauce and toss well. Serve immediately with side dish of grated pecorino cheese.

Penne with Chili Sauce (above) and Pasta with Tomato and Yogurt Sauce (left).

browned all over. Add the tomato paste, salt and pepper to taste, and the stock, and simmer gently for about ¾ hour, until the mixture thickens, stirring occasionally. Add 2 tablespoons sherry, and cook for a further 5 minutes. Meanwhile, place the spaghetti in lots of boiling salted water, and cook for 10 minutes, or until tender but still firm. Drain. Serve with Bolognese sauce on top, and sprinkle with Parmesan cheese.

Fish Ravioli

PREPARATION TIME: 30 minutes	
COOKING TIME: 30 minutes	
OVEN: 350°F (180°C)	
SERVES: 4 people	

Dough:
1¼ cups bread flour
Pinch of salt
3 eggs

Filling:
½ pound sole fillets, or flounder, skinned and boned
2 tbsps breadcrumbs
2 eggs, beaten
1 green onion, finely chopped
1 slice of onion
1 slice of lemon
6 peppercorns
1 bay leaf
1 tbsp lemon juice
1 cup water

Lemon sauce:
2 tbsps butter or margarine
2 tbsps flour
1 cup strained cooking liquid from fish
2 tbsps heavy cream
2 tbsps lemon juice
Salt
Pepper

To make filling:
Pre-heat oven. Wash and dry fish. Place in oven-proof dish with slice of onion, slice of lemon, peppercorns, bay leaf, lemon juice and water. Cover and cook in oven for 20 minutes. Remove fish from liquid, and allow to drain. Strain liquid, and set aside. When fish is cool, beat with the back of a spoon to a pulp. Add eggs, breadcrumbs and green onion, and salt and pepper to taste. Mix well.

This page: Fish Ravioli.

Facing page: Spaghetti Bolognese (top) and Pasta Spirals with Creamy Parsley Sauce (bottom).

Pasta Spirals with Creamy Parsley Sauce

PREPARATION TIME: 5 minutes	
COOKING TIME: 15 minutes	

1 9oz package pasta spirals
2 tbsps butter or margarine
1 tbsp flour
1 cup milk
1 tbsp chopped parsley
1 tbsp lemon juice, or 1 tsp vinegar

Heat butter in pan; when melted, stir in flour. Cook for 1 minute. Remove from heat, and gradually stir in milk. Return to heat, and stir continuously until boiling. Cook for 2 minutes. Meanwhile, cook pasta spirals in lots of boiling salted water for 10 minutes, or until tender but still firm. Rinse in hot water, and drain well. Just before serving, add lemon juice and parsley to sauce, and pour over pasta. Serve immediately.

Spaghetti Bolognese

PREPARATION TIME: 10 minutes	
COOKING TIME: 1 hour 15 minutes	

1 9oz package spaghetti
2 tbsps butter or margarine
1 tbsp olive oil
2 onions, peeled and chopped finely
½ pound ground beef
1 carrot, scraped and chopped finely
¼ cup tomato paste
1 cup brown stock
2 tbsps sherry
Salt and pepper
Parmesan cheese, grated

Heat the butter and oil in a pan and fry the onions and carrot slowly until soft. Increase heat and add the ground beef. Fry for a few minutes, then stir, cooking until meat is

To make dough:

Sift flour into a bowl. Make a well in the center, and add the eggs. Work the flour and eggs together with a spoon, and then knead by hand, until a smooth dough is formed. Leave to rest for 15 minutes. Lightly flour board, and roll out dough thinly into a rectangle. Cut dough in half. Shape the filling into small balls, and set them about 1½" apart on one half of the dough. Place the other half on top, and cut with a ravioli cutter or small pastry cutter. Seal the edges. Cook in batches in a large, wide pan with plenty of boiling salted water until tender – about 8 minutes. Remove carefully with a perforated spoon. Meanwhile, make sauce.

To make sauce:

Melt butter in pan. Stir in flour, and cook for 30 seconds. Draw off heat, and gradually stir in liquid from cooked fish. Return to heat and bring to boil. Simmer for 4 minutes, stirring continuously. Add cream and mix well. Season to taste. Remove from heat, and gradually stir in lemon juice. Do not reboil.

Pour sauce over ravioli and serve immediately.

Ravioli with Ricotta Cheese

PREPARATION TIME: 30 minutes	
COOKING TIME: 20 minutes	
SERVES: 4 people	

Dough:
1¼ cups bread flour
Pinch of salt
3 eggs

Filling:
2 tbsps butter or margarine
½ pound ricotta cheese
¼ cup Parmesan cheese, grated
1 egg yolk
2 tbsps chopped parsley
Salt
Pepper

Tomato sauce:
1 large can (about 2 cups) plum tomatoes
1 tsp basil
1 tbsp olive oil
2 strips bacon
1 tbsp heavy cream
1 small onion, peeled and chopped
1 bay leaf
1 tbsp flour
Salt
Pepper

To make filling:

Beat the butter to a cream, add egg yolk, and blend well. Beat ricotta cheese to a cream, and add butter-egg mixture gradually until smooth. Add Parmesan cheese and parsley, and salt and pepper to taste. Set aside.

To make dough:

Sift flour in a bowl. Make a well in the center, and add the eggs. Work flour and eggs together with a spoon, and then knead by hand, until a smooth dough is formed. Leave to rest for 15 minutes. Lightly flour board, and roll dough out thinly into a rectangle. Cut dough in half. Shape the filling into small balls and set them about 1½" apart on one half of the dough. Place the other half on top and cut with a ravioli cutter or small pastry cutter. Seal the edges. Cook in batches in a large, wide pan with plenty of boiling salted water until tender – about 8 minutes. Remove carefully with a perforated spoon. Meanwhile, make sauce.

To make sauce:

Heat oil, and fry bacon and onion until golden. Add bay leaf and basil, and stir in flour. Cook for 1 minute, draw off heat, and add tomatoes gradually, stirring continuously. Add salt and pepper to taste. Return to heat and bring to boil. Cook for 5 minutes, then push through a sieve. Stir in cream, and adjust seasoning.

Pour sauce over ravioli. Serve immediately.

Whole-wheat Spaghetti with Walnuts and Parsley

PREPARATION TIME: 10 minutes	
COOKING TIME: 10 minutes	

1 9oz package whole-wheat spaghetti
4 tbsps parsley
2 tbsps walnuts
¼ cup olive oil
2 cloves garlic, peeled
Salt and pepper
¼ cup grated Parmesan or pecorino cheese

Fry garlic gently in oil for 2 minutes. Set oil aside to cool. Wash parsley and remove stalks. Finely chop parsley, walnuts and garlic in a food processor with a metal blade, or in a blender. When chopped well, add cooled oil in a thin stream. Turn mixture into a bowl, mix in grated cheese, and add salt and pepper to taste. Cook spaghetti in a large pan of boiling salted water for 10 minutes or until tender but still firm. Drain. Serve with sauce tossed through. Serve with a side dish of grated Parmesan or pecorino cheese.

Tagliatelle with Bacon and Tomato Sauce

PREPARATION TIME: 15 minutes	
COOKING TIME: 15 minutes	

¾ pound red tagliatelle
1 onion, peeled and finely chopped
6 slices bacon, cut into strips

and fry until lightly colored. Draw off heat, and stir in flour with a metal spoon. Return to heat and cook for 2 minutes. Remove from heat, and add wine, and return to heat, stirring until boiling. Add hare, cover pan, and simmer gently for about 1 hour, until hare is tender. Add salt and pepper to taste. When sauce is ready, cook spaghetti in lots of boiling salted water for about 10 minutes, or until tender but still firm. Rinse in hot water, and drain. Serve with hare sauce on top. Serve immediately.

Brasciole with Tagliatelle

PREPARATION TIME:	15 minutes
COOKING TIME:	25 minutes
SERVES:	4 people

½ pound tagliatelle
4 veal steaks, or cutlets
4 thin slices ham
4 tbsps grated Parmesan cheese
2 tbsps butter or margarine
2 small cans (about 2 cups) tomato
   sauce
Salt
Pepper

Pound veal steaks out thinly. Place a slice of ham on the top of each steak. Sprinkle a tablespoon of the Parmesan cheese over each steak, and freshly-ground black pepper. Roll up, and tie gently with string at each end and in the middle. Heat butter in a pan, and add veal rolls. Cook gently until lightly browned all over. Add tomato sauce, and cover. Cook for 15 minutes. Meanwhile, cook tagliatelle in plenty of boiling salted water for 10 minutes, or until tender but still firm. Rinse in hot water, and drain. Cut veal rolls into 1" rounds. Toss tagliatelle together with tomato sauce, and top with veal rolls and grated Parmesan cheese. Serve immediately.

Tagliatelle with Garlic and Oil

PREPARATION TIME: 5 minutes
COOKING TIME: 10 minutes

1 9oz package green tagliatelle
½ cup olive oil
3 cloves garlic, crushed
2 tbsps chopped parsley
Salt and pepper

Cook the tagliatelle in lots of boiling salted water for 10 minutes, or until tender but still firm, stirring occasionally. Meanwhile, make the sauce. Heat the oil in a pan and, when warm, add peeled, crushed garlic. Fry gently until golden brown. Add chopped parsley, and salt and pepper to taste. Drain tagliatelle. Add sauce, and toss to coat well. Serve hot.

Farfalle with Tomato Sauce

PREPARATION TIME: 10 minutes
COOKING TIME: 30 minutes

1 9oz package farfalle
4 small cans (about 4 cups) tomato
  sauce
1 tbsp olive oil
1 onion, peeled and sliced
2 cloves garlic, crushed
½ tsp dry basil
Salt and pepper
2 tbsps chopped fresh basil or
  chopped parsley
Parmesan cheese, grated

Heat oil in a deep pan. Add garlic and onion, and cook until softened. Add dry basil, and cook for 30 seconds. Add tomato sauce; season with salt and pepper. Bring to the boil, reduce heat, and simmer, uncovered, for about 20 minutes, or until sauce is reduced by half and stir in the fresh parsley or basil.

Meanwhile, cook the pasta in a large pan of boiling salted water, until tender but still firm – about 10 minutes. Rinse in hot water, and drain well. Toss sauce through pasta. Serve with grated Parmesan cheese. Serve immediately.

Pasta Shells with Mushroom Sauce

PREPARATION TIME: 5 minutes
COOKING TIME: 15 minutes

1 9oz package pasta shells
½ pound mushrooms
2 tbsps butter or margarine
1 tbsp flour
1 cup milk
Salt and pepper

Rinse the mushrooms and chop them roughly. Melt butter in a saucepan and add mushrooms. Fry for 5 minutes, stirring occasionally. Stir in the flour and cook for 1 minute. Draw off the heat, and add milk gradually, stirring continuously. Bring to the boil and cook for 3 minutes. Season with salt and pepper. Meanwhile, cook

This page: Tagliatelle with Garlic and Oil (top) and Spaghetti with Basil Sauce (Pesto) (bottom).

Facing page: Pasta Shells with Mushroom Sauce (top) and Farfalle with Tomato Sauce (bottom).

the pasta shells in lots of boiling salted water for 10 minutes, or until tender but still firm. Rinse in hot water and drain well. Place in a warmed serving dish, and pour over mushroom sauce. Serve immediately.

Tortellini

PREPARATION TIME: 30 minutes
COOKING TIME: 15 minutes
SERVES: 4 people

Dough:
1¼ cups bread flour
Pinch of salt
3 eggs
1 tbsp water
1 tbsp oil

Filling:
1 cooked chicken breast, finely diced
2 spinach leaves, stalks removed, cooked and chopped finely
2 tbsps ham, finely diced
1 tbsp grated Parmesan cheese
2 tbsps cream cheese
1 egg, beaten
Salt
Pepper

Sauce:
1 cup cream
¼ pound mushrooms, cleaned and sliced
¼ cup Parmesan cheese, grated
1 tbsp chopped parsley
Salt
Pepper

To make filling:
Beat the cream cheese until soft and smooth. Add chicken, ham, spinach and Parmesan cheese, and mix well. Add egg gradually, and salt and pepper to taste. Set aside.

To make dough:
Sift flour and salt onto a board. Make a well in the center. Mix water, oil and lightly-beaten egg together, and gradually pour into well, working in the flour with the other hand, a little at a time. Continue until the mixture comes together in a firm ball of dough. Knead on a lightly-floured board for 5 minutes, or until smooth and elastic. Put into a bowl, cover with a cloth, and let stand for 15 minutes. Roll dough out on a lightly-floured board as thinly as possible. Using a 2" cutter, cut out rounds. Put ½ teaspoon of filling into the center of each round. Fold in half, pressing edges together firmly. Wrap around forefinger, and press ends together. Cook in batches in a large pan, in plenty of boiling salted water for about 10 minutes until tender, stirring occasionally.

To make sauce:
Meanwhile, gently heat cream in a pan. Add mushrooms, Parmesan cheese, parsley, and salt and pepper to taste. Gently cook for 3 minutes.

Toss sauce together with tortellini. Serve immediately, sprinkled with parsley.

Pasta Shells with Walnuts and Cream Cheese

PREPARATION TIME: 5 minutes
COOKING TIME: 15 minutes

1 9oz package pasta shells
1 tbsp olive oil
1 clove garlic, crushed
1 tbsp oregano
2 tbsps butter or margarine
⅓ cup milk
1¼ pound package cream cheese
½ cup walnuts, chopped very finely (keep a few aside to decorate)
⅓ cup cream
Parmesan cheese, grated
Salt and pepper

Heat oil in a pan. Add crushed garlic and oregano, and cook for 1 minute. Add butter, cream cheese, chopped walnuts, and salt and pepper to taste. Stir, and leave to simmer gently for 5 minutes. Meanwhile, cook pasta shells in plenty of boiling salted water for 10 minutes, or until shells are tender but still firm. Drain in a colander, shaking to remove any trapped water. Put into warmed serving dish. Remove sauce from heat; add cream, and stir. Pour over shells, and toss to coat evenly. Garnish with walnut halves. Serve immediately with grated Parmesan cheese.

Spinach Ravioli

PREPARATION TIME: 30 minutes
COOKING TIME: 20 minutes
SERVES: 4 people

Dough:
1¼ cups bread flour
Pinch of salt
3 eggs

Filling:
1 cup cooked spinach
2 tbsps butter or margarine
¼ cup Parmesan cheese, grated
Pinch of grated nutmeg
1 egg, beaten
Salt
Pepper

Cream cheese sauce:
2 tbsps butter or margarine
1 tbsp flour
1 cup milk
1 tsp Dijon mustard
2 tbsps grated Parmesan cheese

To make filling:
Chop spinach and heat in a pan. Beat butter into spinach. Add Parmesan cheese, nutmeg, and salt and freshly-ground black pepper to taste. Finally mix in the beaten egg well.

To make dough:
Sift flour in a bowl; make a well in the center, and add the eggs. Work flour and eggs together with a spoon, and then knead by hand, until a smooth dough is formed. Leave to rest for 15 minutes. Lightly flour board, and roll out dough thinly into a rectangle. Cut dough in half. Shape the filling into small balls, and set them about 1½" apart on one half of the dough. Place the other half on top, and cut with a ravioli cutter or small pastry cutter. Seal the edges. Cook in batches in a large, wide pan with plenty of boiling salted water until tender – about 8 minutes. Remove carefully with a perforated spoon. Meanwhile, make sauce.

To make sauce:
Heat butter in pan. Stir in flour and cook for 30 seconds. Draw off heat, and stir milk in gradually. Bring to boil and simmer for 3 minutes, stirring continuously. Add mustard, and half the cheese, and seasoning to taste.

Pour sauce over ravioli, and serve immediately with remaining cheese sprinkled over the top.

Spaghetti with Basil Sauce (Pesto)

PREPARATION TIME: 5 minutes
COOKING TIME: 15 minutes

1 9oz package spaghetti
2 cups fresh basil leaves

Tagliatelle with Butter and Cheese (top) and Pasta Shells with Walnuts and Cream Sauce (right).

2 tbsps pine nuts
¼ cup olive oil
2 cloves garlic, peeled
Salt and pepper
3 tbsps Parmesan or pecorino cheese, grated

Garnish:
Fresh basil

Wash basil and remove leaves, discarding stems. Heat 1 tablespoon of oil over a low temperature. Add garlic and pine nuts, and cook until pine nuts are a light golden brown. Drain. Finely chop basil leaves, pine nuts and garlic in a food processor with a metal blade, or in a blender. When smooth, add remaining oil in a thin stream, blending continuously. Turn mixture into a bowl; mix in grated cheese, and add salt and pepper to taste. Meanwhile, cook spaghetti in a large pan of boiling salted water for 10 minutes, or until just tender. Drain, and serve with basil sauce tossed through. Serve with side dish of grated cheese. Garnish with fresh basil.

Penne with Spicy Chili Sauce

PREPARATION TIME: 15 minutes

COOKING TIME: 40 minutes

1 9oz package penne
1 onion, peeled and chopped
1 large can (about 2 cups) plum tomatoes
2 red chili peppers, seeds removed, and chopped finely
2 cloves garlic, crushed
1 tbsp olive oil
4 strips bacon, diced
¼ cup pecorino cheese, grated
2 green onions, chopped
Salt and pepper

Garnish:

4 green onions (cut into 2 inch strips. Keeping one end intact, cut into strips. Soak in chilled water until the flower has opened).

Chop tomatoes, removing seeds by straining juice. Heat oil in a pan, and fry garlic, onion and bacon gently for 10 minutes. Add tomato, chili peppers and chopped green onions, and half the cheese, and salt and pepper to taste. Cook, uncovered, for 20 minutes. 10 minutes before sauce is ready, cook the penne in lots of boiling salted water for 10 minutes, or until tender but still firm. Rinse under hot water, and drain well. Put into a warmed serving dish, and toss together with half the sauce. Pour remaining sauce on top, and garnish with green onion flowers, and remaining cheese if desired. Serve at once.

Tagliatelle with Butter and Cheese

PREPARATION TIME: 5 minutes

COOKING TIME: 15 minutes

¾ pound tagliatelle – ¼ pound each yellow, green and red tagliatelle
3 tbsps butter
¼ cup Parmesan cheese, grated
⅓ cup heavy cream
Salt and pepper

Cook the tagliatelle in a large pan of boiling salted water for 10 minutes, or until just tender. Drain. Meanwhile, put the butter and cream in a pan, and stir over a low heat until butter has melted. Remove from heat, add half the grated cheese, and salt and pepper to taste. Stir into tagliatelle and

serve immediately with remaining cheese on top.

Pasta Spirals with Peas and Tomatoes

PREPARATION TIME: 5 minutes

COOKING TIME: 15 minutes

1 9oz package pasta spirals
1½ cups peas
1 tsp sugar
1 large can (about 2 cups) plum tomatoes, chopped
1 tsp basil
2 tbsps butter or margarine
Salt and pepper

Cook pasta spirals in plenty of boiling salted water for 10 minutes or until tender. Drain. Meanwhile, cook peas in boiling water with a pinch of salt and a teaspoon of sugar. Melt butter in a pan. Add basil, and cook for 30 seconds.

Add tomatoes and their juice. When hot, add pasta spirals and peas, and salt and pepper to taste. Toss together. Serve immediately.

Spaghetti with Egg, Bacon and Mushroom

PREPARATION TIME: 10 minutes

COOKING TIME: 15 minutes

1 9oz package spaghetti
1 cup mushrooms, sliced
4 strips bacon, diced
4 tbsps butter or margarine
¼ cup Parmesan cheese, grated
2 eggs, hard-boiled and chopped finely
1 tbsp chopped parsley
Salt and pepper

Melt half the butter in a frying-pan. Add mushrooms and bacon, and cook for 10 minutes over a

moderate heat, until bacon is crisp. Meanwhile, cook the spaghetti in lots of boiling salted water until tender but still firm – about 10 minutes. Drain. Return to pan. Add rest of butter, salt and lots of freshly-ground black pepper, and the mushroom and bacon. Toss together. Serve with hard-boiled eggs sprinkled on top, and parsley if desired. Serve grated Parmesan cheese separately.

This page: Pasta Spirals with Peas and Tomatoes.

Facing page: Spaghetti with Egg, Bacon and Mushroom (top) and Penne with Spicy Chili Sauce (bottom).

Salads and Stuffed Vegetables

dressing, and toss together.

Niçoise Salad

PREPARATION TIME: 15 minutes

COOKING TIME: 15 minutes

SERVES: 4 people

1½ cups penne
3 tomatoes, quartered
¼ pound green beans, cooked
½ cucumber, cut into batons
1 7oz can tuna fish, drained and
  flaked
12 black olives, halved, with stones
  removed
6-8 anchovy fillets, drained, and
  soaked in milk if desired
½ cup bottled oil and vinegar
  dressing

Bean Salad

PREPARATION TIME: 10 minutes

COOKING TIME: 15 minutes

SERVES: 4 people

3 cups macaroni
1 large can red kidney beans, drained
4 strips bacon, diced

1 onion, peeled and chopped
2 sticks celery, sliced diagonally
1-2 tbsps wine vinegar
3-4 tbsps olive oil
1 tsp chopped parsley
Salt
Pepper

Cook macaroni in plenty of salted boiling water for 10 minutes, or until tender but still firm. Rinse in cold water and drain well.
Heat frying pan, and sauté bacon in its own fat until crisp. Add onion, and cook until soft. Mix vinegar, oil and parsley, and season well. Add bacon, onion, kidney beans and celery to macaroni. Pour over

Nicoise Salad (far left), Bean Salad (left) and Tuna and Tomato Salad (below).

Cook penne in lots of boiling salted water until tender but still firm. Rinse in cold water; drain, and leave to dry. Put flaked tuna in the base of a salad dish. Toss pasta together with tomatoes, cucumber, green beans, olives, and anchovies, and then pour over oil and vinegar dressing. Mix together well.

Tuna and Tomato Salad

PREPARATION TIME: 10 minutes

COOKING TIME: 15 minutes

SERVES: 4 people

3 cups pasta shells
1 7oz can tuna fish, flaked
6 tomatoes
1 tbsp fresh chopped basil or marjoram, or 1 tsp dried basil or oregano
6 tbsps vinaigrette dressing

Mix herbs with vinaigrette dressing. Cook pasta shells in a large saucepan of boiling salted water until tender – about 10 minutes. Rinse with cold water, and drain, shaking off excess water. Toss with 3 tablespoons of vinaigrette dressing. Leave to cool. Meanwhile, slice enough of the tomatoes to arrange around the outside of the serving-dish. Chop the rest, and pour the remaining vinaigrette dressing over them, and place in the center of the dish. Add tuna to the pasta shells, and toss gently. Serve in the center of the dish over the chopped tomatoes.

Stuffed Eggplant

PREPARATION TIME: 15 minutes

COOKING TIME: 1 hour

OVEN: 350°F (180°C)
          400°F (200°C)

4 small or 2 large eggplants
¾ cup macaroni
½ pound bacon, diced
1 green pepper, cored and diced
1 yellow pepper, cored and diced
2 tomatoes, skin removed, chopped and seeds removed
2 tbsps butter
½ tsp chili powder
1 tbsp tomato paste
1 small onion, peeled and chopped
1 clove garlic, crushed
¼ cup Gruyère or Cheddar cheese, grated
1 tbsp breadcrumbs
Salt and pepper

Cook macaroni in plenty of boiling, salted water for 10 minutes, or until

tender but still firm. Rinse in cold water, and drain well. Wrap eggplants in baking foil, and bake in a moderate oven (350°F, 180°C) for 30 minutes. Cut eggplants in half lengthwise. Scoop out the pulp, leaving ½ inch of thickness on the skin. Chop pulp. Heat butter in a pan. Add onion and garlic, and cook until transparent. Add bacon and peppers and fry for 5 minutes. Then add eggplant pulp, tomato, tomato paste, chili powder, and salt and pepper. Cook a further 3 minutes. Stir in macaroni, and fill the scooped-out eggplant halves with the mixture. Top with grated

cheese and breadcrumbs, and brown under a broiler or in a quick oven (400°F, 800°C). Serve immediately.

Gianfottere Salad

PREPARATION TIME: 40 minutes

COOKING TIME: 30 minutes

SERVES: 4 people

3 cups pasta spirals
1 eggplant
1 zucchini
1 sweet red pepper

1 green pepper
2 tomatoes
1 onion
4 tbsps olive oil
1 clove garlic
Salt
Pepper

Cut eggplant into ½″ slices. Sprinkle with salt and leave for 30

This page: Gianfottere Salad.

Facing page: Stuffed Eggplant.

minutes. Skin the tomatoes by putting them into boiling water for 20 seconds, and then rinsing in cold water, and peeling skins off. Chop roughly. Cut zucchini into ½" slices. Remove cores and seeds from peppers, and chop roughly. Peel and chop onion. Heat 3 tbsps olive oil in pan, and fry onion gently until transparent, but not colored. Meanwhile, rinse salt from eggplant, and pat dry with absorbent paper. Chop roughly. Add eggplant, zucchini, peppers, tomatoes and garlic to onion, and fry gently for 20 minutes. Season with salt and pepper. Allow to cool.

Meanwhile, cook pasta spirals in a lot of boiling salted water for 10 minutes, or until tender but still firm. Rinse in cold water and drain well, and toss in remaining 1 tbsp olive oil. Toss vegetables together with pasta spirals.

Stuffed Zucchini

PREPARATION TIME: 15 minutes
COOKING TIME: 30 minutes
OVEN: 400°F (200°C)

4 zucchini
¾ cup soup pasta
2 tomatoes, skin removed, chopped, and seeds removed
2 tbsps butter or margarine
¼ pound ground beef
1 small onion, peeled and chopped
2 cloves garlic, crushed
¼ cup Gruyère or Cheddar cheese, grated
1 tbsp breadcrumbs
1 tsp tomato paste
Salt and pepper

Cook pasta in lots of boiling salted water for 5 minutes or until tender. Rinse in cold water and drain well. Meanwhile, put zucchini in a pan and cover with cold water. Bring to the boil and cook gently for 3 minutes. Rinse under cold water. Cut zucchini in half lengthwise. Carefully scoop out the pulp, leaving ½ inch thickness on skin. Chop pulp. Heat butter in a frying-pan. Add garlic and onion, and fry gently until transparent. Increase heat and add ground beef. Cook for 5 minutes, turning often until meat is well browned. Stir in tomato paste and salt and pepper to taste. Add zucchini pulp, tomatoes and pasta, and cook for 2 minutes. Spoon into zucchini shells. Sprinkle top with grated cheese and breadcrumbs, and brown under a broiler or in a fast oven. Serve immediately.

Stuffed Tomatoes

PREPARATION TIME: 10 minutes
COOKING TIME: 20 minutes
OVEN: 350°F (180°C)

4 large ripe tomatoes
1 pound fresh spinach
¼ tsp grated nutmeg
2 tbsps butter, creamed
¾ cup soup pasta
1 tbsp heavy cream
1 clove garlic, crushed
1 tbsp Gruyère or Cheddar cheese, grated
4 anchovies, sliced
Salt and pepper

Cut tops off tomatoes, and carefully scoop out the insides with a teaspoon. Wash spinach well and remove stalks. Cook gently in a large saucepan, without added water, until spinach is soft. Chop very finely, or blend in a food processor. Meanwhile, cook pasta for 5 minutes, or until tender. Rinse and drain well. Mix with the spinach. Add butter, cream, nutmeg and garlic, and season well. Fill each tomato and top with cheese and anchovies. Bake in a moderate oven for 10 minutes. Serve immediately.

Mushroom Salad

PREPARATION TIME: 1 hour 10 minutes
COOKING TIME: 15 minutes
SERVES: 4 people

3 cups farfalle (pasta butterflies/bows)
1 cup mushrooms, sliced
5 tbsps olive oil
Juice of 2 lemons
1 tsp fresh chopped basil
1 tsp fresh chopped parsley
Salt
Pepper

Mix oil together with lemon juice and fresh herbs. Put the sliced mushrooms into a bowl, and pour over 4 tbsps of the dressing. Leave for 1 hour. Cook the pasta in a large saucepan of boiling salted water for 10 minutes, or until tender. Rinse in cold water, and drain. Toss with the rest of the dressing, and leave to cool. Fold mushrooms and pasta together gently, adding salt and freshly-ground black pepper to taste. Sprinkle with parsley.

Shrimp Salad

PREPARATION TIME: 10 minutes
COOKING TIME: 15 minutes
SERVES: 4 people

3 cups pasta shells
½ pound shrimp, shelled and deveined
½ cup mayonnaise
Juice of 1 lemon
1 tsp paprika
Salt
Pepper
1 lettuce
1 cucumber, sliced

Cook the pasta in plenty of boiling salted water for 10 minutes, or until tender. Drain, and rinse under cold water. Shake off excess water; put into a bowl, and pour over lemon juice. Leave to cool. Mix paprika into mayonnaise. Add to shrimp, and toss. Arrange a bed of lettuce leaves and sliced cucumber in a dish, and pile pasta in center. Pile shrimp on top.
(This can also be made with flaked crab meat or salmon).

Stuffed Zucchini (above right) and Stuffed Tomatoes (top).

Curried Shrimp Salad

PREPARATION TIME: 10 minutes	
COOKING TIME: 20 minutes	
SERVES: 4 people	

1½ cups soup pasta
½ pound shrimp, shelled and de-
    veined
1 tsp paprika
Juice of ½ a lemon
1½ tsp curry powder
1 tsp tomato paste
2 tbsps olive oil
1 small onion, peeled and chopped
1 clove garlic, crushed
½ cup water
2 slices lemon
1 tsp apricot jam
1 cup mayonnaise
Salt
Pepper

Heat oil, and fry garlic and onion
gently until soft but not colored.
Add curry powder and paprika,
and cook for 2 minutes. Stir in
tomato paste and water. Add
lemon slices, and salt and pepper to
taste. Cook slowly for 10 minutes;
stir in jam, and bring to the boil,
simmering for 2 minutes. Strain and
leave to cool. Add mayonnaise.
Meanwhile, cook pasta in plenty of
boiling salted water for 10 minutes,
or until tender but still firm. Rinse
under cold water and drain well.
Toss in lemon juice, and put in
serving-dish. Arrange shrimp on
top, and pour over curry sauce.
Toss well. Sprinkle with paprika.

Zucchini Salad

PREPARATION TIME: 15 minutes	
COOKING TIME: 15 minutes	
SERVES: 4 people	

2 cups elbow macaroni
4 zucchini, sliced thinly
2 tomatoes, chopped
8 stuffed green olives, sliced
6 tbsps vinaigrette dressing

Cook pasta in lots of boiling salted
water for 10 minutes, or until
tender but still firm. Rinse in cold
water, and drain well. Mix with
3 tablespoons vinaigrette dressing.
Leave to cool. Meanwhile, cook the
zucchini gently in boiling, lightly-
salted water, until just tender but
still crisp. Drain, and flush with
cold water. Leave to cool. Mix
together pasta, zucchini, tomatoes
and stuffed olives, and 3 tablespoons vinaigrette dressing. Serve
chilled.

Mexican Chicken Salad

PREPARATION TIME: 10 minutes	
COOKING TIME: 15 minutes	
SERVES: 4 people	

1¼ cups soup pasta shells
½ pound or 1 cup cooked chicken,
    shredded
1 7oz can corn, drained
1 stick celery, sliced
1 sweet red pepper, cored, seeds
    removed, and diced
1 green pepper, cored, seeds removed,
    and diced

Dressing:
1 tbsp mayonnaise
2 tbsps vinegar
Salt
Pepper

Cook pasta in plenty of boiling
salted water until just tender. Drain
well, and leave to cool. Meanwhile,
combine mayonnaise with vinegar
and salt and pepper to taste. When
the pasta is cool, add chicken, corn,
celery and peppers. Toss well and
serve with dressing.

**This page: Mexican Chicken
Salad.**

**Facing page: Curried Shrimp
Salad (top) and Zucchini
Salad (bottom).**

Variety Meats

Pasta Spirals with Kidneys in Madeira Sauce

PREPARATION TIME: 15 minutes

COOKING TIME: 30 minutes

1 9oz package pasta spirals
6 lambs' kidneys
1 tbsp flour
Salt and pepper
1 small onion, peeled and chopped finely
1 clove garlic, crushed
4 tbsps butter or margarine
¾ cup mushrooms, sliced
6 strips bacon, diced
½ cup Madeira wine, or dry white wine

Split and remove hard core from kidneys. Cut in half lengthwise. Add salt and pepper to flour and mix well. Coat kidneys in seasoned flour. Heat butter in pan; add onion and garlic, and cook until soft and translucent. Add kidneys and brown on both sides. Add bacon and mushroom, and cook, stirring frequently, for 3 minutes. Add wine, and bring to the boil. Simmer gently for 15 minutes, or until kidneys are tender. Adjust seasoning. Meanwhile, cook the pasta spirals in plenty of boiling salted water for 10 minutes, or until tender but still firm. Rinse in hot water and drain well. Serve immediately, with kidney sauce on top.

Tagliatelle with Creamy Liver Sauce

PREPARATION TIME: 10 minutes

COOKING TIME: 15 minutes

1 9oz package tagliatelle
4 tbsps olive oil
2 medium onions, peeled and sliced
1 clove garlic, crushed
¾ cup mushrooms, sliced
1 pound chicken livers, cleaned and sliced
⅓ cup cream
2 eggs, beaten
1 tbsp chopped parsley
Salt and pepper

In a large frying pan, cook onions and garlic gently in oil until softened. Add mushrooms and cook for 3 minutes. Add chicken livers to onions and mushrooms, and cook until lightly browned. Remove from heat and stir in cream. Return to low heat, and cook, uncovered, for further 2

Tagliatelle with Creamy Liver Sauce (left) and Pasta Spirals with Kidneys in Madeira Sauce (below).

minutes. Remove from heat, and stir in lightly beaten eggs. Season with salt and pepper to taste. Meanwhile, cook the tagliatelle in plenty of boiling salted water for 10 minutes, or until tender but still firm, stirring occasionally. Drain tagliatelle, toss in oil and black pepper. Serve sauce over tagliatelle and sprinkle with parsley.

Baked and Broiled Dishes

Cannelloni

PREPARATION TIME:	10 minutes
COOKING TIME:	1 hour
OVEN:	350°F (180°C)
SERVES:	4 people

12 cannelloni shells
2 tbsps Parmesan cheese, grated
1 tbsp oil

Filling:
1lb ground beef
1 tbsp olive oil
1 onion, peeled and chopped
2 cloves garlic, crushed
1 cup chopped, cooked spinach
½ tsp oregano
½ tsp basil
1 tsp tomato paste
4 tbsps cream
1 egg, lightly beaten
Salt and pepper to taste

Tomato sauce:
1 tbsp olive oil
1 onion, peeled and chopped
1 clove garlic, crushed
2 small cans (about 2 cups) tomato
  sauce
2 tbsps tomato paste
Salt
Pepper

Béchamel sauce:
1 slice of onion
3 peppercorns
1 small bay leaf
1 cup milk
2 tbsps butter or margarine
2 tbsps flour
Salt
Pepper

To make filling:
Heat oil in pan, and fry garlic and onion gently until soft and transparent. Add meat and cook, stirring continuously, until well browned. Drain off any fat, add tomato paste, basil and oregano, and cook gently for 15 minutes. Add spinach, egg and cream, and salt and pepper to taste. Cook cannelloni in a large pan of boiling salted water for 15-20 minutes, until tender. Rinse in hot water and drain. Fill carefully with meat mixture, using a pastry bag with a wide, plain tube, or a teaspoon.

To make tomato sauce:
Heat oil in pan. Add onion and garlic, and cook gently until transparent. Add tomato sauce to the pan with tomato paste and salt and pepper to taste. Bring to boil, and then simmer for 5 minutes. Set aside.

To make Béchamel sauce:
Put milk in pan with onion, peppercorns and bay leaf. Heat gently for 1 minute, taking care not to boil, and set aside to cool for 5 minutes. Strain. Melt butter in

This page: Shrimp Crespelle.

Facing page: Cannelloni with Tomato and Cheese (top) and Cannelloni (bottom).

Crespelle with Tuna (left) and Crespelle with Chicken and Tongue (below).

pan. Remove from heat and stir in flour. Gradually add cool milk, and bring to boil, stirring continuously, until sauce thickens. Add seasoning.

Spread tomato sauce on the base of an oven-proof dish. Lay cannelloni on top, and cover with Béchamel sauce. Sprinkle with grated cheese, and bake in a moderate oven for 30 minutes. Serve immediately.

Shrimp Crespelle

PREPARATION TIME: 40 minutes
COOKING TIME: 30 minutes
OVEN: 375°F (190°C)
SERVES: 4 people

12 crespelle:
3 eggs
¾ cup flour
Pinch of salt
1 cup water
½ tbsp olive oil
2 tbsps butter or margarine, melted

Filling:
1 cup shrimp, washed, peeled and deveined
2 tbsps butter or margarine
1 tbsp flour
1 cup milk
Juice of 1 lemon
Salt
Pepper

Garnish:
1 lemon, cut into slices

To make crespelle:
Sift flour with a pinch of salt. Break eggs into a bowl, and whisk. Add flour gradually, whisking all the time until the mixture is smooth. Add water, and stir in well. Add oil, and mix. Cover bowl with damp cloth, and leave in a cool place for 30 minutes.
Heat a crêpe pan or 7" frying pan. Grease lightly with melted butter, and put a tablespoon of batter in the center. Roll the pan to coat the surface evenly. Fry until crespelle is brown on the underside. Loosen edge with a spatula; turn over and brown the other side. Stack and wrap in a clean cloth until needed.

To make filling:
Heat butter in pan; stir in flour, and cook for 1 minute. Remove from heat, and gradually stir in milk. Return to heat, and bring to the boil. Allow to simmer for 3 minutes. Stir in lemon juice and add salt and pepper to taste. Add half the sauce to shrimp. Place one crespelle in an oven-proof dish, and add a spoon of shrimp mixture. Cover with one crespelle, and repeat, finishing with a crespelle on top. Bake in a pre-heated oven for 10 minutes. When ready to serve, cover with remaining sauce. Garnish with lemon slices. Serve immediately.

Crespelle with Chicken and Tongue

PREPARATION TIME: 40 minutes
COOKING TIME: 20 minutes
OVEN: 450°F (230°C)
SERVES: 4 people

10 crespelle:
3 eggs
¾ cup flour
Pinch of salt
1 cup water
½ tsp olive oil
2 tbsps butter or margarine, melted

Filling:
¼ pound chicken, cooked and shredded
¼ pound tongue, cut into strips

Béchamel sauce:
2 tbsps butter or margarine
1 tbsp flour
1 cup milk
To infuse:
4 peppercorns
1 bay leaf
Slice of onion
Salt
Pepper

To make crespelle:
Sift flour with a pinch of salt. Break eggs into a bowl, and whisk. Add flour gradually, whisking all the time until the mixture is smooth. Add water and stir in well. Add oil, and mix. Cover bowl with a damp cloth, and leave in a cool place for 30 minutes.
Heat a crêpe pan, or 7" frying pan. Grease lightly with melted butter, and put a good tablespoon of batter in the center. Roll the pan to coat the surface evenly. Fry until crespelle is brown on the underside. Loosen edge with a spatula; turn over and brown the other side. Stack and wrap in a clean cloth until needed.

To make Béchamel sauce:
Warm milk with peppercorns, bay leaf and slice of onion. Remove from heat, and let stand for 5 minutes. Strain. Heat butter in pan. Stir in flour and cook for 1 minute. Remove from heat, and gradually stir in two-thirds of the milk. Return to heat, and stir continuously until boiling. Simmer for 3 minutes. Add salt and pepper to taste. Put half of the sauce in a bowl, and add the chicken and tongue. Mix together. Beat remaining milk into remaining sauce.

Lay 1 crespelle on a plate and top with a layer of chicken and tongue. Cover with another crespelle, and continue, finishing with a crespelle.

Pour over sauce, and bake in pre-heated oven for 10 minutes. Serve immediately.

Crespelle with Tuna

PREPARATION TIME: 40 minutes
COOKING TIME: 30 minutes
SERVES: 4 people

12 crespelle:
3 eggs
¾ cup flour
Pinch of salt
1 cup water
½ tbsp olive oil
2 tbsps butter or margarine, melted

Filling:
1 cup tuna fish, drained
3 tbsps mayonnaise
1 tbsp tomato paste

Tomato sauce:
2 small cans (about 2 cups) tomato sauce
½ tsp basil
1 clove garlic, crushed
1 onion, peeled and chopped
1 tbsp butter or margarine
2 tbsps chopped parsley
Salt
Pepper

To make crespelle:
Sift the flour with a pinch of salt. Break eggs into a bowl, and whisk. Add flour gradually, whisking all the time, until the mixture is smooth. Stir in water, and mix oil in well. Cover bowl with a damp cloth, and leave in a cool place for 30 minutes.
Heat a crêpe pan, or 7" frying pan. Grease lightly with melted butter, and put a good tablespoon of batter in the center. Roll the pan to coat the surface evenly. Fry until crespelle is brown on the underside. Loosen edge with a spatula; turn over and brown on the other side. Stack and wrap in a clean cloth until needed.

To make sauce:
Heat butter in pan, and gently fry garlic and basil for 30 seconds. Add onion, and fry until transparent. Add tomato sauce, and cook for 10 minutes. Add salt, and freshly-ground black pepper, to taste, and parsley if desired.

To make filling:
Flake tuna fish, and put into a bowl. Mix mayonnaise and tomato paste, and stir into tuna fish. Divide mixture equally between crespelle, placing mixture at one end, and rolling up. Place in an oven-proof dish. Pour over tomato sauce, and cook under a broiler for 5 minutes. Serve immediately.

Cook the macaroni in plenty of boiling salted water for 10 minutes, or until tender but still firm. Rinse in hot water and drain well. Meanwhile, melt the butter in a pan. Stir in the flour and cook for 1 minute. Remove from heat, and gradually stir in the milk. Return to heat and bring to the boil. Simmer for 3 minutes, stirring continuously. Stir in the mustard, anchovies, and half the cheese. Season with salt and pepper to taste. Stir in the macaroni, and pour into an oven-proof dish. Sprinkle the remaining cheese over the top, and make a latticework with the remaining anchovies. Brown under a hot grill. Serve immediately.

Macaroni with Creamy Chicken Sauce

PREPARATION TIME: 5 minutes	
COOKING TIME: 20 minutes	
SERVES: 4 people	

1 9oz package macaroni
4 tbsps butter or margarine
2 tbsps flour
2 cups milk
2 chicken breasts
1 tbsp olive oil
½ cup Cheddar cheese, grated
Salt
Pepper

Heat oil in a frying pan, and gently fry chicken for 10 minutes, or until cooked through. When cool, shred chicken. Cook macaroni in plenty of boiling salted water for 10 minutes, or until tender but still firm. Rinse in hot water. Drain well. Meanwhile, heat the butter in a pan, and stir in the flour, and cook for 1 minute. Draw off the heat and gradually add the milk, stirring all the time. Bring the sauce to the boil, stirring continuously, and cook for 3 minutes. Add the chicken, macaroni, and salt and pepper to taste, and mix well. Pour mixture into an oven-proof dish, and sprinkle with cheese on top. Cook under a broiler until golden brown. Serve immediately.

Macaroni Cheese with Anchovies

PREPARATION TIME: 5 minutes	
COOKING TIME: 15 minutes	
SERVES: 4 people	

1 9oz package macaroni
4 tbsps butter or margarine
3 tbsps flour
2 cups milk
½ tsp dry mustard
¾ cup Gruyère or Cheddar cheese, grated

6-8 anchovy fillets
Salt
Pepper

Drain anchovies, and set enough aside to slice to make a thin lattice over the dish. Chop the rest finely.

This page: Macaroni Cheese with Anchovies.

Facing page: Macaroni with Creamy Chicken Sauce (top) and Italian Casserole (bottom).

Italian Casserole

PREPARATION TIME: 15 minutes

COOKING TIME: 40 minutes

OVEN: 350°F (180°C)

SERVES: 4 people

1 cup small macaroni
2 tbsps butter or margarine
1 clove garlic, crushed
1 onion, peeled and chopped
1 large can (about 2 cups) plum
   tomatoes
1 tbsp tomato paste
1 sweet red pepper, cored, seeds
   removed, and chopped roughly
1 green pepper, cored, seeds removed,
   and chopped roughly
10 black olives, halved, and stones
   removed
¼ pound Mozzarella cheese, sliced
   thinly
½ pound salami, cut into chunks
Salt
Pepper

Cook the macaroni in plenty of
boiling salted water for 10 minutes,
or until tender but still firm. Rinse
under hot water and drain well.
Place in a shallow, oven-proof dish.
Meanwhile, heat butter in pan, and
fry onion and garlic gently until
soft. Add undrained tomatoes,
tomato paste, red and green
peppers, salami and olives, and stir
well. Simmer uncovered for
5 minutes. Season with salt and
pepper. Pour over the macaroni,
stir, and cover with the sliced
cheese. Bake uncovered in a
moderate oven for 20 minutes,
until cheese has melted. Serve
immediately.

Macaroni Cheese with Frankfurters

PREPARATION TIME: 10 minutes

COOKING TIME: 20 minutes

SERVES: 4 people

1 9oz package macaroni
4 tbsps butter or margarine
3 tbsps flour
2 cups milk
1 tsp dry mustard
⅓ cup Cheddar cheese, grated
8 Frankfurters
Salt
Pepper

Garnish:
1 pimento, cut into strips

Poach the Frankfurters for 5-8
minutes. Remove skins and, when
cold, cut into diagonal slices. Cook
macaroni in plenty of boiling salted
water for about 10 minutes, or until
tender but still firm. Rinse in hot
water, and drain well. Meanwhile,
melt the butter in a pan. Stir in the
flour, and cook for 1 minute. Draw
off heat, and gradually add milk,
stirring all the time. Bring to the
boil, stirring continuously, and
cook for 3 minutes. Add Frankfurters, grated cheese, mustard, and
salt and pepper to taste. Stir well.
Add macaroni, and mix in well.
Pour mixture into an oven-proof
dish, and sprinkle the remaining
cheese over the top. Make a lattice
of pimento, and cook under a pre-
heated grill until golden brown.
Serve immediately.

Pastitsio

PREPARATION TIME: 10 minutes

COOKING TIME: 1 hour

OVEN: 375°F (190°C)

SERVES: 4 people

1 9oz package macaroni
4 tbsps butter or margarine
¼ cup Parmesan cheese, grated
Pinch of grated nutmeg
2 eggs, beaten
1 medium onion, peeled and chopped
1 clove garlic, crushed
1 pound ground beef
2 tbsps tomato paste
¼ cup red wine
½ cup beef stock
2 tbsps chopped parsley
2 tbsps plain flour
½ cup milk
Salt
Pepper

Set oven. Cook macaroni in plenty
of boiling salted water for
10 minutes, or until tender but still
firm. Rinse under hot water. Drain.
Put one-third of the butter in the
pan and return macaroni to it. Add
half the cheese, nutmeg, and salt
and pepper to taste. Leave to cool.
Mix in half the beaten egg, and put
aside. Melt half of the remaining
butter in a pan, and fry onion and
garlic gently until onion is soft.
Increase temperature and add meat,
and fry until browned. Add tomato
paste, stock, parsley and wine, and
season with salt and pepper.
Simmer for 20 minutes. In a small
pan, melt the rest of the butter. Stir
in the flour and cook for
30 seconds. Remove from heat,
and stir in milk. Bring to boil,
stirring continuously, until the
sauce thickens. Beat in the
remaining egg and season to taste.
Spoon half the macaroni into a
serving-dish and cover with the
meat sauce. Put on another layer of
macaroni and smooth over. Pour
over white sauce, and sprinkle with
remaining cheese, and bake in the
oven for 30 minutes until golden
brown. Serve immediately.

Cannelloni with Tomato and Cheese

PREPARATION TIME: 10 minutes

COOKING TIME: 40 minutes

OVEN: 400°F (210°C)

SERVES: 4 people

12 cannelloni shells

Filling:
1 15oz can plum tomatoes
1 tbsp tomato paste
1 tbsp oregano or basil
½ cup ricotta cheese
½ cup Parmesan cheese, grated
Salt
Pepper

Sauce:
2 small cans (about 2 cups) tomato
   sauce
1 onion, peeled and chopped
1 tbsp olive oil
1 tbsp grated Parmesan cheese
1 tbsp cornstarch
Salt
Pepper

Cook cannelloni shells in a large
pan of boiling salted water for 15-20
minutes until tender. Rinse in hot
water and drain well.

**Pastitsio (above) and
Macaroni Cheese with
Frankfurters (right).**

To make filling:
Meanwhile, chop tomatoes and remove pips. Set juice aside for sauce. Beat ricotta cheese until smooth. Add tomato paste, oregano or basil, and Parmesan cheese, and beat well. Finally, stir in chopped tomato and salt and pepper to taste. With a teaspoon, or a pastry bag with a wide, plain tube, fill the cannelloni shells. Place in an oven-proof dish.

To make sauce:
Heat oil in a saucepan, and cook onion gently until transparent. Add tomato sauce to the saucepan. Mix the cornstarch with the reserved tomato juice and add to the pan. Bring to the boil and cook for 3 minutes, stirring continuously. Add salt and pepper to taste. Pour over the cannelloni, and sprinkle with cheese. Place in a hot oven, or under a broiler for 10 minutes or until heated through. Serve immediately.

Spinach Crespelle

PREPARATION TIME:	45 minutes
COOKING TIME:	30 minutes
SERVES:	4 people

12 crespelle:
3 eggs
¾ cup flour
Pinch of salt
1 cup water
½ tbsp olive oil
2 tbsps butter or margarine, melted

Filling:
1 8oz package cream cheese
1 8oz package frozen spinach, thawed
2 tbsps cream
¼ cup Parmesan cheese, grated
½ tsp grated nutmeg
2 tbsps butter or margarine
Salt
Pepper

To make crespelle:
Sift flour with a pinch of salt. Break eggs into a bowl, and whisk. Add flour gradually, whisking all the time until the mixture is smooth. Add water, and stir in well. Add oil, and mix in. Cover bowl with a damp cloth, and leave in a cool place for 30 minutes. Heat a crêpe pan, or 7″ frying pan. Grease lightly with melted butter, and put a good tablespoon batter in the center. Roll the pan to coat the surface

evenly. Fry until crespelle is brown on the underside. Loosen edge with a spatula, and turn over and brown on the other side. Stack and wrap in a clean cloth until needed.

To make filling:
Cook spinach for 3 minutes in a pan of boiling water. Drain and chop, and set aside. Beat cream cheese and cream together until smooth. Add nutmeg and half the cheese, and salt and pepper to taste, and mix in well. Mix spinach into cream cheese mixture. Divide equally between 12 crespelle, placing mixture at one end, and rolling up. Place in an oven-proof dish, and dot with butter over the top. Sprinkle with Parmesan cheese, and place under a broiler for 5 minutes, or until browning lightly on top. Serve immediately.

Crespelle with Bolognese Sauce Filling

PREPARATION TIME:	45 minutes
COOKING TIME:	1 hour 15 minutes
SERVES:	4 people

12 crespelle:
3 eggs
¾ cup flour
Pinch of salt
1 cup water
1½ tsp olive oil
2 tbsps butter or margarine, melted

Bolognese Sauce:
2 tbsps butter or margarine
1 tbsp olive oil
2 onions, peeled and chopped finely
½ pound ground beef
1 carrot, scraped and chopped finely
4 tbsps tomato paste
1 cup brown stock
2 tbsps sherry
Salt
Pepper

Tomato Sauce:
1 large can (about 2 cups) plum tomatoes
½ tsp basil
1 clove garlic, crushed
1 onion, peeled and chopped
1 tbsp butter
Salt
Pepper

To make Bolognese sauce:
Heat the butter and oil in a pan, and fry the onions and carrot slowly until soft. Increase heat, and add the ground beef. Fry for a few minutes, then stir, cooking until

meat is browned all over. Add the tomato paste, stock, and salt and pepper to taste, and simmer gently for about ¾ hour, until the mixture thickens, stirring occasionally. Add 2 tablespoons sherry, and cook for a further 5 minutes.

To make crespelle:
Sift the flour with a pinch of salt. Break the eggs into a bowl, and whisk. Add the flour gradually, whisking all the time until the mixture is smooth. Add water, and stir in well. Add oil, and mix. Cover bowl with a damp cloth, and leave in a cool place for 30 minutes.

Heat a crêpe pan, or 7″ frying pan. Grease lightly with the melted butter, and put a good tablespoon of batter in the center. Roll the pan to coat the surface evenly. Fry until crespelle is brown on the underside. Loosen edge with a spatula, and turn over and brown the other side. Stack and wrap in a clean cloth until needed.

To make tomato sauce:
Heat butter in pan, and gently fry garlic and basil for 30 seconds. Add onion, and fry until transparent. Add tomatoes, and cook for 10 minutes. Strain, and return to pan. Add salt and freshly-ground black pepper to taste.

Lay crespelle out, and put 2 heaped tablespoons Bolognese sauce filling at one end of each. Roll up, and place in an oven-proof dish. Repeat until all crespelle have been filled. Put into a hot oven or under a broiler for 5 minutes. Re-heat tomato sauce, and pour over just before serving. Serve immediately.

Spinach Lasagne

PREPARATION TIME:	10 minutes
COOKING TIME:	30 minutes
OVEN:	400°F (200°C)
SERVES:	4 people

8 green lasagne noodles

Spinach sauce:
4 tbsps butter or margarine
1½ cups frozen spinach, thawed and chopped finely
Pinch of ground nutmeg
3 tbsps flour
½ cup milk
Salt
Pepper

Mornay sauce:
2 tbsps butter or margarine
2 tbsps flour
1 cup milk
⅓ cup Parmesan cheese, grated
1 tsp Dijon mustard
Salt

To make spinach sauce:
Heat butter in pan, stir in flour and cook for 30 seconds. Draw off heat, and stir in milk gradually. Return to heat, and bring to the boil, stirring continuously. Cook for 3 minutes. Add spinach, nutmeg, and salt and pepper to taste. Set aside.

Cook spinach lasagne in lots of boiling salted water for 10 minutes, or until tender. Rinse in cold water, and drain carefully. Dry on a clean cloth.

To make Mornay sauce:
Heat butter in pan and stir in flour, cooking for 30 seconds. Remove from heat, and stir in milk. Return to heat, stirring continuously, until boiling. Continue stirring, and simmer for 3 minutes. Draw off heat, and add mustard and two-thirds of cheese, and salt to taste.

Grease an oven-proof baking dish. Line the base with a layer of lasagne, followed by some of the spinach mixture, and a layer of cheese sauce. Repeat the process, finishing with a layer of lasagne and with a covering of cheese sauce. Sprinkle with the remaining cheese. Bake in a hot oven until golden on top. Serve immediately.

Curried Tuna Cannelloni

PREPARATION TIME:	15 minutes
COOKING TIME:	45 minutes
OVEN:	350°F (180°C)
SERVES:	4 people

12 cannelloni shells

Filling:
2 tbsps butter or margarine
1 onion, peeled and chopped
1 stick of celery, chopped

Facing page: Crespelle with Bolognese Sauce Filling (top) and Spinach Crespelle (bottom).

½ cup mushrooms, cleaned and
    chopped
1 tbsp flour
1 tsp curry powder
½ cup milk
⅓ cup soured cream
⅓ cup mayonnaise
1 egg, lightly beaten
1 7oz can tuna fish
3 shallots, peeled and chopped
Salt
Pepper

Topping:
4 tbsps breadcrumbs
¼ cup Cheddar cheese, grated
2 tbsps butter or margarine

Cook cannelloni shells in a large
pan of boiling salted water for 15-20
minutes until tender. Rinse in hot
water and drain well. Meanwhile,
melt butter in saucepan. Fry onion
until transparent, add mushrooms
and celery, and fry for 5 minutes.
Add curry powder and flour, and
fry until light golden brown. Draw
off the heat, and gradually add milk,
stirring continuously. Return to
heat and bring to the boil. Cook for
3 minutes, stirring all the time. Add
soured cream, mayonnaise, and
undrained flaked tuna. Season with
salt and pepper and stir until sauce
boils. Simmer for 3 minutes. Add

shallots and egg, and mix well.
Spoon mixture into cannelloni
shells, and place in an oven-proof
dish. Sprinkle over a mixture of
breadcrumbs and cheese, and dot
with butter or margarine. Bake in a
moderate oven for 20 minutes.
Serve immediately.

Crab Cannelloni

PREPARATION TIME:	10 minutes
COOKING TIME:	40 minutes
OVEN:	400°F (200°C)
SERVES:	4 people

This page: Spinach Lasagne.

**Facing page: Curried Tuna
Cannelloni (top) and Crab
Cannelloni (bottom).**

12 cannelloni shells

Filling:
½ pound fresh crab meat (or frozen
    crab meat, thawed)
2 tbsps butter or margarine
3 shallots, peeled and chopped

½ tsp Worcestershire sauce
1 tsp Dijon mustard
Salt
Pepper

Mornay sauce:
2 tbsps butter or margarine
2 tbsps flour
1¼ cups milk
¼ cup Cheddar or Parmesan cheese, grated
Salt
Pepper

Cook cannelloni shells in a large pan of boiling salted water for 15-20 minutes until tender. Rinse in hot water and drain well. Meanwhile, heat butter in pan. Add shallots, crab meat, Worcestershire sauce, mustard, salt and pepper, and stir until heated through. Fill cannelloni shells with crab mixture, using a pastry bag with a wide, plain tube, or a teaspoon. Place in an oven-proof dish.

To make Mornay sauce:
Heat butter in pan, and stir in flour. Remove from heat and gradually add milk. Return to heat, and bring to boil. Cook for 3 minutes, stirring continuously. Stir in half the cheese until it melts. Do not reboil. Season with salt and pepper. Pour over the cannelloni and sprinkle with remaining cheese. Place in a hot oven, or under a broiler until golden brown. Serve immediately.

Lasagne Rolls

PREPARATION TIME: 5 minutes
COOKING TIME: 15 minutes
SERVES: 4 people

8 lasagne noodles
½ pound boned chicken breasts
2 tbsps butter or margarine
¼ cup Gruyère or Cheddar cheese, grated
1 tbsp flour
½ cup milk
¼ cup mushrooms, sliced
2 tsps oil
Salt
Pepper

In a large saucepan, fill two-thirds with boiling salted water and 2 teaspoons oil. Bring to the boil. Add 1 sheet of lasagne; wait about 2 minutes, and add another sheet. Only cook a few at a time. When tender, remove, and rinse under cold water, and leave to drain. Repeat until all the lasagne is cooked. Meanwhile, wash and slice mushrooms, and slice chicken. Put half the butter in a small frying pan, and fry the mushrooms and chicken. In a small saucepan, melt the rest of the butter. Add the flour, and cook for a minute. Remove from the heat, and add the milk. Mix well and bring to the boil. Cook for 3 minutes. Add sauce to chicken and mushrooms, and add half the cheese, mixing well. Add salt and pepper to taste. Spread out lasagne, and spread one-eighth mixture at one end of each. Roll up each piece of lasagne, and put into an oven-proof dish. Sprinkle with remaining cheese, and put under a broiler until golden brown. Serve immediately.

Lasagne

PREPARATION TIME: 10 minutes
COOKING TIME: 45 minutes
OVEN: 400°F (200°C)
SERVES: 4 people

8 lasagne noodles

Meat sauce:
4 tbsps butter or margarine
1 carrot, diced
1 celery stick, diced
1 onion, peeled and diced
¼ pound ground beef
1 tsp marjoram
1 tbsp flour
1 tbsp tomato paste
½ cup beef stock
Salt
Pepper

Béchamel sauce:
2 tbsps butter or margarine
2 tbsps flour
1 cup milk
6 peppercorns
1 bay leaf
Slice of onion
Parsley stalks

To make meat sauce:
Heat butter in pan and add onion, celery and carrot. Cook until golden. Add ground beef, and brown well. Stir in flour; add tomato paste, beef stock, marjoram, and salt and pepper. Cook for 15 minutes.

Meanwhile, cook the lasagne in lots of boiling salted water for 10 minutes, or until tender. Rinse in cold water and drain carefully. Lay out on a clean cloth to dry.

To make Béchamel sauce:
Heat milk in a saucepan with peppercorns, slice of onion, bay leaf and parsley stalks. Bring to simmering point and remove from heat. Allow to cool for 5 minutes. Strain. Melt butter in a saucepan. Stir in flour and cook for 30 seconds. Remove from heat and gradually add milk, stirring continuously. Cook for 3 minutes.

Grease an oven-proof baking dish. Line base with a layer of lasagne sheets. Cover with a layer of meat sauce, and a layer of Béchamel sauce. Place another layer of lasagne, repeating until all the ingredients are used, finishing with a layer of lasagne and a layer of Béchamel sauce. Bake in a hot oven until the top is golden. Serve immediately.

Lasagne Rolls (above right) and Lasagne (below right).

Desserts

Vanilla Cream Melba

PREPARATION TIME: 15 minutes

COOKING TIME: 10 minutes

SERVES: 4 people

⅔ cup soup pasta
1½ cups milk
2½ tbsps brown sugar
½ cup cream, lightly whipped
Few drops vanilla extract
1 can peach halves
1 tsp cinnamon

Melba sauce:
1 cup raspberries
2 tbsps powdered sugar

Cook pasta in milk and sugar until soft. Stir regularly, being careful not to allow it to boil over. Draw off heat and stir in vanilla extract. Pour pasta into a bowl to cool. When cool, fold in cream. Chill. Meanwhile, make Melba sauce. Push raspberries through a strainer. Mix in powdered sugar to desired thickness and taste. Serve pasta with peach halves and Melba sauce. Dust with cinnamon if desired.

Black Cherry Ravioli with Soured Cream Sauce

PREPARATION TIME: 30 minutes

COOKING TIME: 15 minutes

SERVES: 4 people

Dough:
1¾ cups bread flour
1 tbsp sugar
3 eggs

Large can dark, sweet cherries, stoned
¼ cup sugar
1 tsp cornstarch
½ cup soured cream
½ cup heavy cream

Strain the cherries and reserve the juice. Make dough by sifting flour and sugar in a bowl. Make a well in the center and add lightly-beaten eggs. Work flour and eggs together with a spoon, and then by hand, until a smooth dough is formed. Knead gently. Lightly flour board, and roll dough out thinly into a rectangle. Cut dough in half. Put well-drained cherries about 1½" apart on the dough. Place the other half on top, and cut with a small glass or pastry cutter. Seal well around edges with the back of a fork. Boil plenty of water in a large saucepan, and drop in cherry pasta. Cook for about 10 minutes, or until they rise to the surface. Remove with a slotted spoon and keep warm. Keep 2 tablespoons cherry juice aside. Mix 1 tablespoon cherry

This page: Black Cherry Ravioli with Soured Cream Sauce.

Facing page: Vanilla Cream Melba (top) and Chocolate Cream Helène (bottom).

juice with cornstarch; mix remaining juice with sugar and set over heat. Add cornstarch mixture, and heat until it thickens. Meanwhile mix soured cream and heavy cream together, and marble 1 tablespoon of cherry juice through it. Pour hot, thickened cherry juice over cherry ravioli. Serve hot with cream sauce.

Chocolate Cream Helène

PREPARATION TIME: 15 minutes

COOKING TIME: 10 minutes

SERVES: 4 people

⅔ cup soup pasta
1½ cups milk
2½ tbsps sugar
½ cup cream, lightly whipped
1 tsp cocoa
1 tbsp hot water
1 large can pear halves

Garnish:
Chocolate, grated

Cook pasta in milk and sugar until soft. Stir regularly, being careful not to allow it to boil over. Meanwhile, dissolve cocoa in hot water, and stir into pasta. Pour pasta into a bowl to cool. When cool, fold in lightly-whipped cream. Chill. Serve with pear halves, and a sprinkling of grated chocolate.

Honey Vermicelli

PREPARATION TIME: 1 hour

COOKING TIME: 15 minutes

SERVES: 4 people

½ pound vermicelli
4 tbsps butter
3 tbsps clear honey
2 tsps sesame seeds
¾ tsp ground cinnamon

Sauce:
½ cup heavy cream
½ cup soured cream

Cook vermicelli in boiling salted water for 5 minutes or until tender, stirring regularly with a fork to separate noodles. Drain, and spread out to dry on a wire tray covered with absorbent paper or a tea-towel. Leave for about an hour. Make sauce by mixing soured cream and heavy cream together. Melt butter in frying pan. Add sesame seeds, and fry until lightly golden. Stir in honey, cinnamon and vermicelli, and heat through. Serve hot, topped with cream sauce.

Cream Cheese Margherita

PREPARATION TIME: 1 hour

COOKING TIME: 10 minutes

SERVES: 4 people

¾ cup soup pasta
½ cup light cream
8oz package cream cheese
½ tsp ground cinnamon
4 tbsps sugar
4 tbsps golden raisins
Juice and grated rind of ½ a lemon

Garnish:
1 tbsp sliced almonds
Lemon peel, cut into slivers

Soak raisins in lemon juice for about 1 hour. Meanwhile, cook the pasta in plenty of boiling, lightly-salted water until tender, stirring occasionally. Work the cream cheese, sugar and cream together until smooth. Beat in grated lemon rind and cinnamon. Fold in pasta and raisins. Divide between individual dessert glasses or small dishes, and cover top with sliced almond and slivers of lemon peel. Chill.

Honey Vermicelli (top right) and Cream Cheese Margherita (right).

Index